I CAN READ ABOUT

WHALES
AND DOLPHINS

Written by J. I. Anderson   Illustrated by Judith Fringuello

Troll Associates

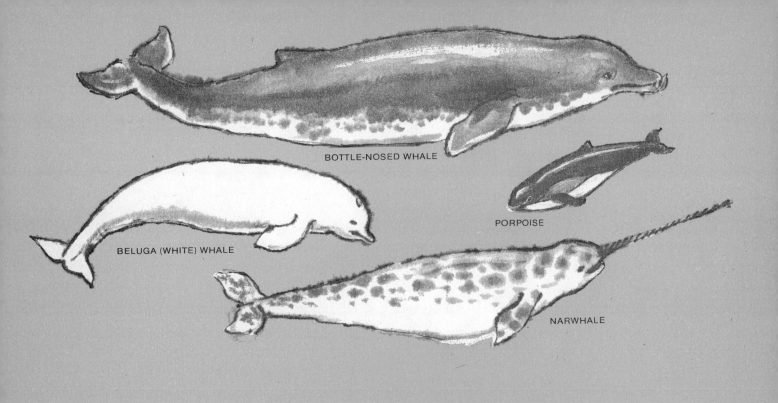

BOTTLE-NOSED WHALE

PORPOISE

BELUGA (WHITE) WHALE

NARWHALE

Many strange and wonderful
creatures live in the sea.

Some are beautiful.
Some are unusual.

Some live deep down,
near the dark bottom.

Some are giant monsters.
Others are very tiny.
Many tiny creatures become food
for the bigger ones.

These bigger creatures then become food for others!
The biggest creature in the sea is the whale.
And of all the animals, the blue whale is largest.

Whales are much bigger
than elephants.

Whales look like fish,
but are really mammals.
Do you know the difference?

Even dinosaurs were not
as large as whales.

Fish have scales. Whales have smooth skin.

Fish are cold-blooded. Their body temperature changes
with the temperature of the water. But whales are warm-blooded.
They need protection from the cold. Under their skin,
whales have a thick blanket of fat, called blubber.
Blubber keeps whales warm while they swim in ice-cold water.

Whales are good swimmers. They flap
their big, flat tails up and down. They use
their flippers for steering and balancing.

Whales have lungs, and must breathe air.
They can dive deep, but soon they must come up
to the surface for fresh air. Some whales
can stay underwater for over an hour.

Look! A whale is spouting.
He forces out the warm, exhaled air
through two blowholes on top of his head.
When this warm air
meets the cold sea air,
it looks like steam.

The whale blows and blows until all the old air is out,
and his lungs are full of fresh air.

Then, with a giant splash of his tail,
he dives deep under the sea.
His blowholes shut tight
to keep the water out.

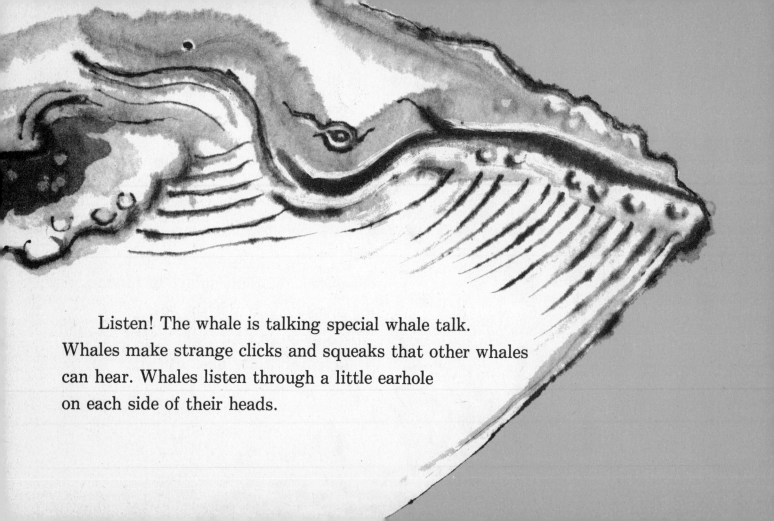

Listen! The whale is talking special whale talk.
Whales make strange clicks and squeaks that other whales
can hear. Whales listen through a little earhole
on each side of their heads.

Scientists think that whales find their way in the water
by using a kind of echo, called sonar. The sound of
their clicks and squeaks travels through the water
and bounces off objects. When the whale hears the echo,
he knows where these objects are.

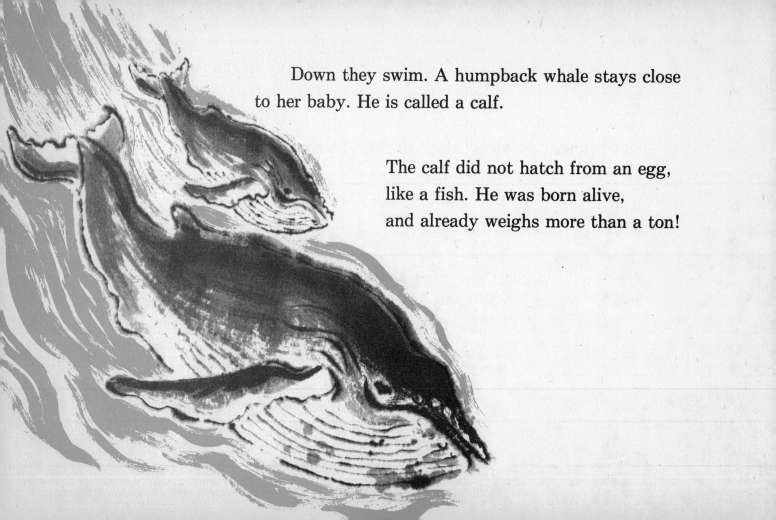

Down they swim. A humpback whale stays close to her baby. He is called a calf.

The calf did not hatch from an egg,
like a fish. He was born alive,
and already weighs more than a ton!

The calf needs his mother's rich milk, just like other baby mammals. When he is 6 or 7 months old, the small whale is able to eat plankton.

Plankton is the name
for tiny plants and animals
floating on the surface of the sea.
Sometimes plankton is so thick
that it covers the water like a
green, yellow or red carpet.

The humpback whale has no teeth. Instead, it has
a giant strainer made of bone in its mouth. This is called a baleen.
When the whale takes a big gulp of seawater, the baleen catches
tiny fish and plankton for the whale to eat.

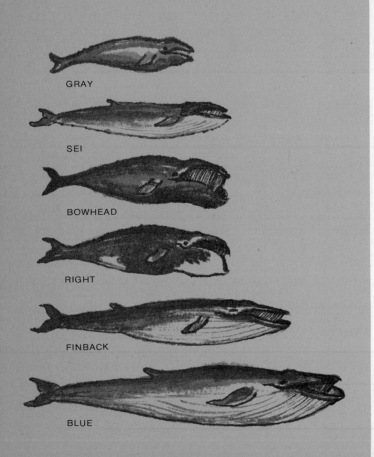

GRAY

SEI

BOWHEAD

RIGHT

FINBACK

BLUE

There are many kinds of baleen whales besides the humpback whale. Plankton is their favorite food. Baleen whales are the giants of the sea. The blue whale, the largest animal in the world, is a baleen whale.

The baleen whales sometimes
travel thousands of miles, just to
find the thickest and best plankton.
In summer, they swim to the cold
waters in the North. In winter, they
make the long trip south,
where the water is warm.

The giant sperm whale is not
a baleen whale. He has teeth
instead of a baleen, and
he does not eat plankton.

The sperm whale has to dive very deep
to find his favorite food—the giant squid.

He grabs the squid in his mouth.
The squid battles back with his
ten long arms, trying to get free.
But the whale usually wins,
and swallows the squid whole.

BOTTLE-NOSED WHALE

PORPOISE

BELUGA (WHITE) WHALE

NARWHALE

There are many kinds of whales that have teeth.
They all eat fish and squid. But none of them
is as big as the sperm whale.

The killer whale is really a dolphin, too. One of the most feared animals in the sea, he will eat almost anything that swims!

Dolphins are members of the whale family.
Some dolphins are even called whales. Pilot whales
are dolphins that can grow as long as 28 feet.
They travel together in large groups called schools.

Even seals and penguins run for their lives when killer whales are near.

Like their cousins the whales, dolphins are
warm-blooded mammals. They have lungs to breathe air.
And their babies are born alive, not hatched from eggs.

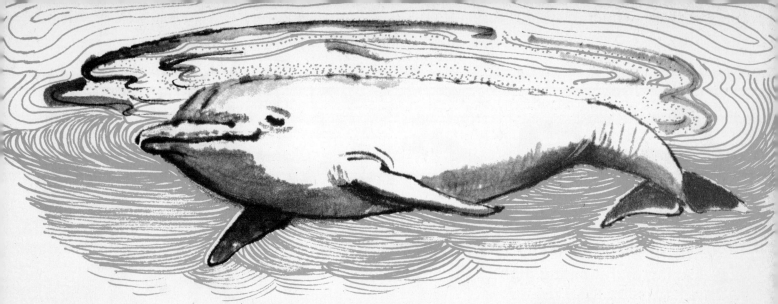

Sometimes a dolphin takes a nap just below the surface of the water. When he needs air, he flips his tail, and up he comes!

He puffs out warm air through his blowhole and breathes in fresh air. Then he goes back to his underwater nap!

Dolphins can swim very fast. They often follow ships,
leaping and jumping high in the air. Many sailors think
they bring good luck.
And some ancient coins and medals
show people playing
in the sea with dolphins.

Most dolphins are playful and friendly. Sometimes they let swimmers ride on their backs, or they save the lives of drowning people. And sometimes they help fishermen by pushing fish into their nets.

Dolphins are very smart.
They can talk to each other
by making clicks, barks,
and whistles.

And they find their way
under the water
by listening for echoes,
just like whales.

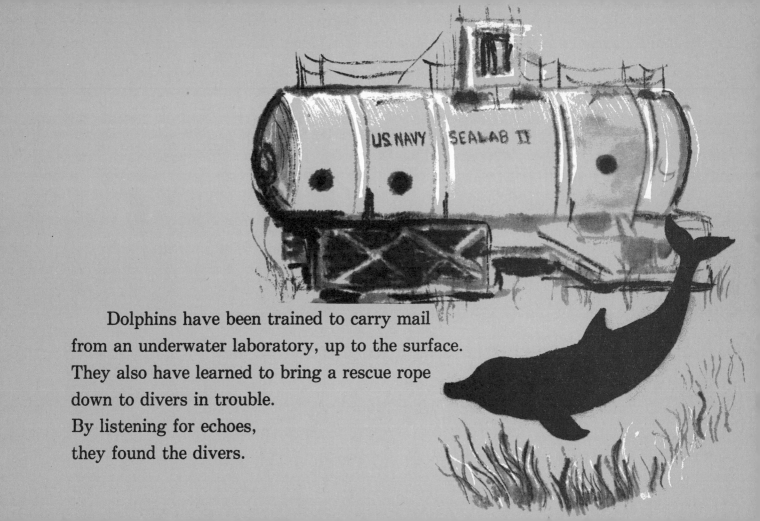

Dolphins have been trained to carry mail
from an underwater laboratory, up to the surface.
They also have learned to bring a rescue rope
down to divers in trouble.
By listening for echoes,
they found the divers.

Dolphins love to show off and do tricks. They can
be trained to jump through a hoop, to catch a stick, and
to play basketball. They can even make up their own games!

A fish or a small squid
is their reward. Watch!
The dolphin leaps high
into the air to catch
the fish! People love
to watch dolphins play,
so they do not usually
hunt or kill these
friendly creatures.

But long ago, men called whalers hunted whales
from small boats. They used long, pointed harpoons.
A long rope was fastened to the harpoon.

As the whale fought hard to get free,
he pulled the men along behind him. This was very dangerous.
The whale could dive down and pull the boat underwater.
Or he could smash the boat with one blow of his powerful tail.

Long ago, whale oil was used for fuel in oil lamps.
If the whalers captured enough whales, they could become
very rich. Almost everything on a whale was valuable.

Later,
hunting whales
became much easier
when harpoons could be shot from a gun.
Men caught more and more whales every year,
until today, there are very few whales left in the sea.

But new laws have been made to protect the whales
from disappearing forever. Maybe soon, the sea will once again
be home to thousands of these gigantic animals.